Building the Acoustic Guitar
Side Bending Machine

*A complete illustrated guide to
building the acoustic guitar side
bending machine from acquisition
of materials to final assembly*

William C. Peterson
Round Rock, Texas

i

Building the Acoustic Guitar Side Bending Machine

ISBN: 979-8-985-9065-2-3

Edited by Elizabeth Peterson

Cover Photo Editor Alejandro Dominguez

Publisher
William C. Peterson

Dedicated to Elizabeth

"The prettiest girl I ever met."

Contents

Introduction

The traditional approach to side bending consisted of a pipe, a heat source, and a skilled craftsman bending the wood around the pipe to create the desired shape. It is still the preferred method of many luthiers. However, the hot pipe method does present some potential pitfalls such as scorched wood, difficulty in controlling the temperature of open flames or other sources of heat, and the skill level necessary to achieve consistent right and left bend profiles, among others. For these reasons, many luthiers and amateur guitar makers have switched to the side bending machine.

The side bending machine greatly simplifies this process. It is straight forward and relatively simple to use and the guitar maker can rely on the side bending machine to consistently deliver uniform results. But side bending machines from luthier supply houses or other sources vary widely in design and can be exceptionally expensive.

You may choose to avoid this expense and make your own side bending machine for a fraction of the cost. The following pages will show you how to produce a professional quality side bending machine. All necessary parts and materials for the build are readily available from building supply outlets and hardware stores. The instructions are fully illustrated and easy to follow. Whether you are building one guitar or one hundred, this side bending machine will serve you well.

William C. Peterson
Round Rock, TX

Gather the Materials

You will need the following components:

3/4" MDF, 8 square feet

1/2" sanded or birch plywood,4 square feet

1" x 2" Poplar, total of 12 feet

3/4" threaded rod, 18 inch length

3/4" hex nuts, 2 each

3/4" lock nuts, 2 each

3/4" washer, 1 each

3/4"drywall screws, 8 each

7/16" threaded rod, 8" length, 2 each

7/16" hex nuts, 4 each

7/16" washers, 8 each

5/16" eye bolts, 7 inch length, 2 each*

5/16" eye bolts, 9 inch length, 2 each*

5/16" washer, 4 each

5/16" utility knob, 4 each

3/8" hardwood dowel

1/2" hardwood dowel

*If these specific lengths are not available, customize the lengths with a 5/16" connector bolt and 5/16" threaded rod cut to the correct length.

Making the Template

The contours of the side bending machine correspond to the shape of the soundboard perimeter. A template of the shape of the guitar's perimeter is used to make the panels and the press block. If you don't have a body template, you can make one.

The process is simple. Begin by laying a guitar on a large sheet of paper and tracing the outline. Rock the edge of the guitar down to the paper as the pencil travels around the perimeter. Once the outline is made, locate the center of the top and bottom and draw a line through the middle dividing the pattern into a right and left hemisphere. Fold the paper in half and cut out the template pattern. The result should deliver a template pattern with right and left hemispheres that mirror each other.

Tape the template pattern onto a piece of 3/8" birch or sanded plywood with blue painter's tape and cut out the template on the band saw. Cut slightly outside the line. Sand the edges down to the line and smooth the edges and curves. Then draw a line down the center of the template.

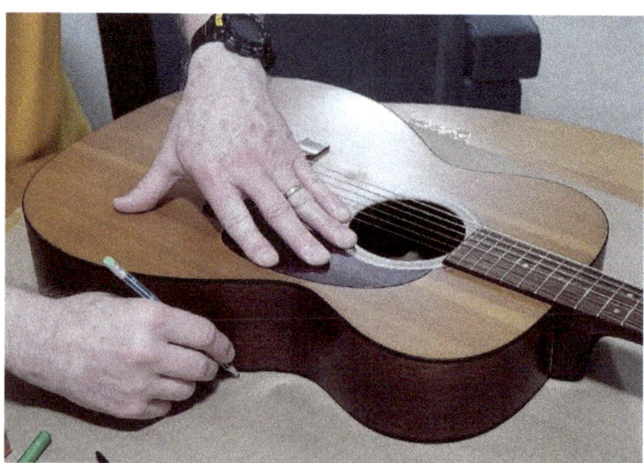

Figure 1 Drawing the template outline

If you are making a bending machine for an OM style guitar the dimensions should be roughly as shown in this diagram. If your measurements differ slightly compared to the diagram, don't panic. These dimensions are not cast in stone. Your template will simply be unique, as are the dimensions of guitars produced by any number of different manufacturers.

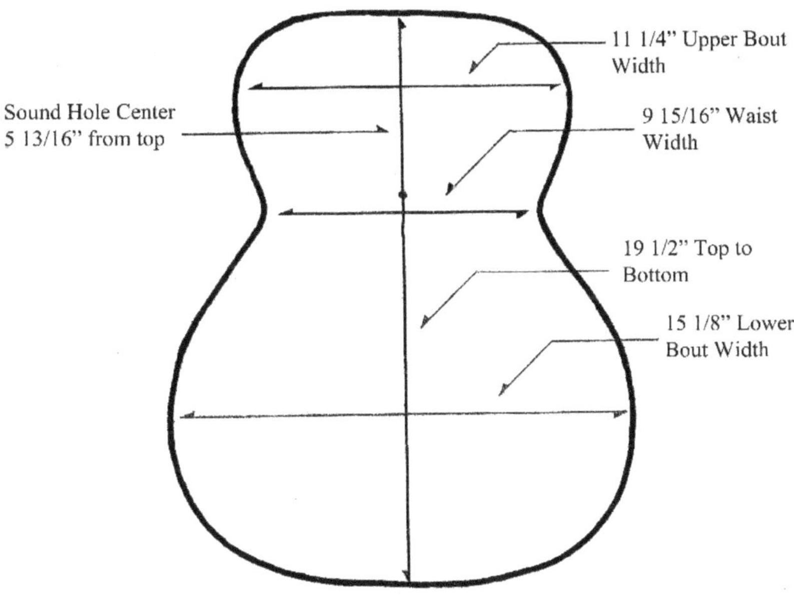

Figure 2 The guitar template

What is important however, is the symmetrical appearance of the left and right sides of the template. This can be checked by taking one half of the pattern and placing it on one side of the template. Then flip the pattern over and compare it to the other side.

Figure 3 Comparing the sides for symmetry

Cut the Main Body Panels

The side bending machine main body consists of four pieces of 3/4" MDF cut to mirror the profile of one half of the guitar body.

Once the template has been made, use the template to mark the outline of the main body panels on the piece of 3/4" MDF. Ensure that the bottom edge of MDF is true and straight. Measure up 3 inches from the bottom and draw a line parallel to the edge. Place the template on the MDF and line up the centerline of the template with the line drawn on the MDF. Mark the outline of the body panel. Use a square to mark a straight line from the bottom of the MDF to the point where the template outline meets the MDF line

Figure 4 Drawing the body panel outline

The result should look like Figure 5.

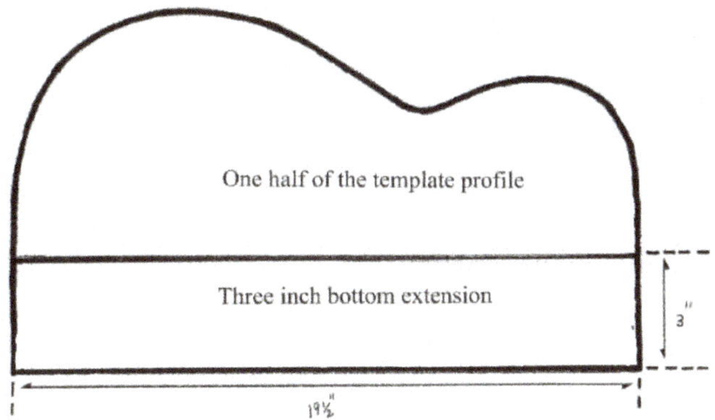

Figure 5 The main body panel profile

Cut out the first body panel on the band saw. Saw outside the line, then sand the excess material down to the line. This panel will be referred to and marked as panel A.

Repeat this process for the remaining three panels and mark them B, C, and D.

Figure 6 Sanding the first panel down to the line

Cut the Body Panel Spacers

The body panels are separated by spacers. There are three long spacers that are 1 1/8" x 3/4" x 12" and six short spacers that are 1 1/8" x 3/4" x 5 1/2". Cut these from poplar stock.

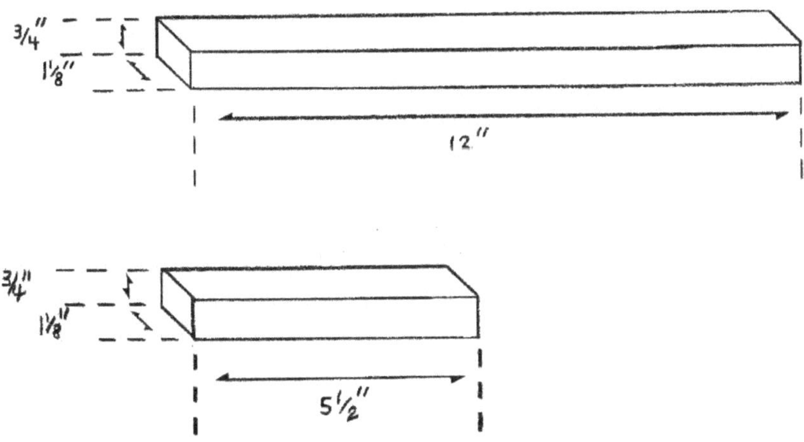

Figure 7 The long and short panel spacers

Cut the Alignment Dowels

Assembly of the body panels is aided by the use of 3/8" x 7 1/2" alignment dowels. Cut three alignment dowels from 3/8" stock.

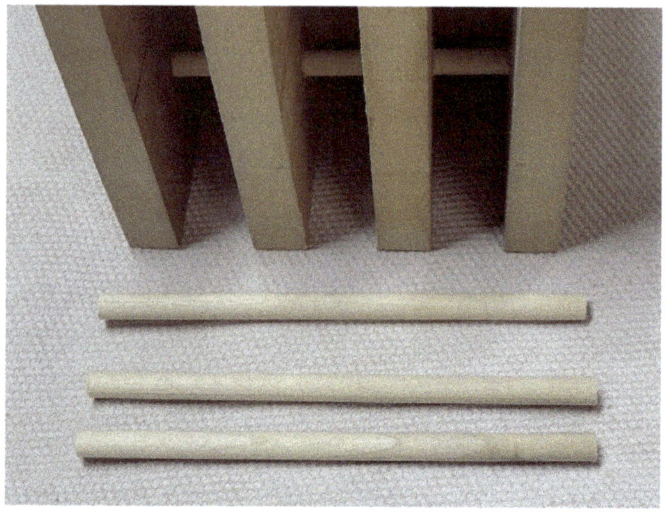

Figure 8 The alignment dowels

Drill the Alignment Dowel
and Hold Down Rod Holes

The location of the alignment holes and the holes for the threaded rods for the eye bolts and hold down blocks are shown in figure 9.

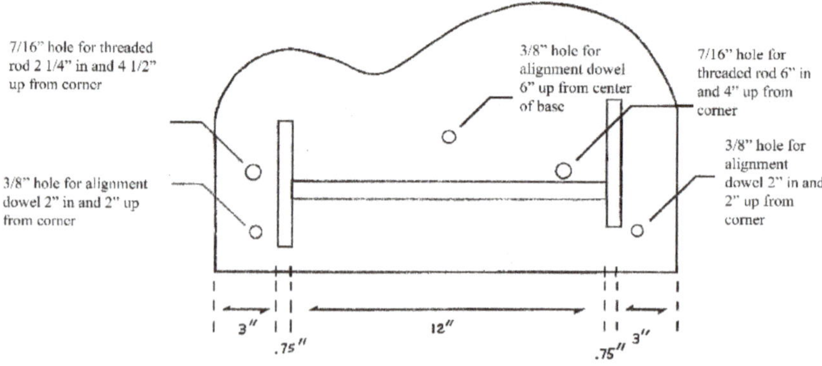

Figure 9 Positions of the alignment dowels and threaded rods

Mark the locations of these holes on panel A. The holes for the threaded rods are made with a 7/16" bit and the alignment dowel holes with a 3/8" bit. Use the drill press to drill these holes as they must be precisely perpendicular to the panel. Use panel A, as a template to drill the holes in the remaining panels. Again, use the drill press to drill these holes to ensure the holes are exactly perpendicular.

Clamp the four panels together and examine the alignment of the holes. Any issues with incorrect hole alignment will need to be addressed at this stage. Precise alignment of the alignment dowel holes is critical. The material will need to be reworked until a satisfactory alignment is achieved.

Once proper alignment is achieved, insert the dowels into the holes and dry fit and clamp the four pieces together without the panel spacers.

Figure 10 The panels dry fit and clamped ready for sanding to ensure a smooth uniform surface

The tolerance between the alignment dowels and the drilled holes will most likely be too tight to enable the pieces to fit together without considerable effort. Buff the dowels with some 100 grit sandpaper and carefully use a rat tail file or a piece of sandpaper wrapped around a screwdriver or 1/4" dowel to slightly enlarge the holes for the alignment dowels as well as the holes for the threaded rods. Be careful not to remove too much material as the alignment dowels need to remain snug in the alignment holes.

Once the pieces are clamped together, examine the upper surfaces of the panels to ensure that they provide a smooth surface.

If imperfections or high spots exist between the panels, place the panels with the alignment dowels in place in a vise and use a sanding block to correct the imperfections. Check your progress with a square to ensure the surface remains square with the sides. Continue until the surface of the four panels is smooth and even. (Figure 10).

Glue the Panel Spacers to Panels B, C, and D

Refer to figure 11 for the correct location of the panel spacers. Glue the spacers to each panel individually. Apply glue to only one side of the spacer bar and ensure that the spacers are glued to the side of the panel that will face the adjoining panel. Use white wood glue to glue the spacers to the panels, then clamp and allow the glue to dry.

This step should result in 3 separate panels with spacers glued to the side that will face the adjoining panel when assembled. The main body width when assembled will be 6.375" wide. Therefore, be sure to align the spacer properly with the glue applied to the 3/4" side and the 1.125" width creating the space between the panels.

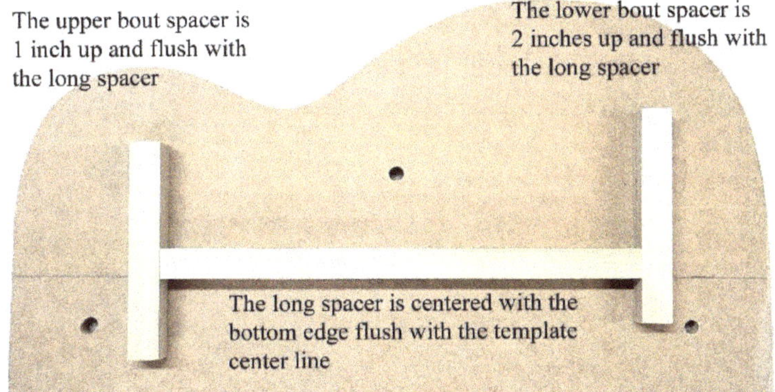

Figure 11 The position of the panel spacers

Dry Fit the Panels,
Then Glue Up the Machine Body

Dry fit the panels with the alignment dowels and panel spacers in place. Check for square and that the machine body sits flat on the work surface. (Figure 12).

Figure 12 Dry fitting the panels

If there are no issues, disassemble the body and apply glue to the spacers and alignment dowel holes. Then assemble the body with the alignment rods and glue up with white glue, clamp and allow the glue to dry.

Figure 13 Gluing up the panels, spacers, and alignment dowels

Fabricate a Press Block Handle

Fashion a handle for the press assembly from 3/4" poplar stock. The handle will be secured to the 3/4 inch threaded rod of the press assembly sandwiched between a hex nut and a lock nut and fixed with two part epoxy. Use the drill press to drill the 3/4 inch hole for the threaded rod to ensure a perfectly perpendicular hole.

A sample handle design is shown below. The handle has a diameter of 6 inches and made by marking the circle perimeter with a compass. Cut the basic shape with the band saw and create the spokes with a scroll saw or coping saw. (Figure 14).

Figure 14 A sample side bending machine handle

Fabricate the Towers

Cut two tower blanks from 1/2 inch sanded or birch
plywood. The dimensions of the tower blanks are 7 3/8" x 24".

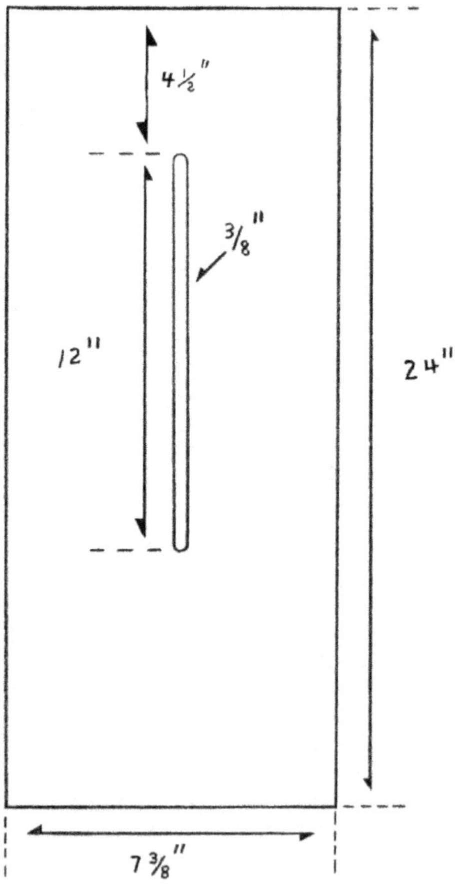

Figure 15 The tower blank dimensions

Rout Out the Press Block Channels

Ensure that the tower blank is square, then rout the press block channel. The press block channel guides the press block up and down the tower and is 3/8" wide and 12" long. The channel is centered on the tower blank and begins 4 1/2" from the top of the blank.

Figure 16 Routing the tower channel

Draw in the Tower Perimeter

Draw in the tower perimeter as shown in figure 17. The stabilizing dowels and screws will be dealt with during the assembly process.

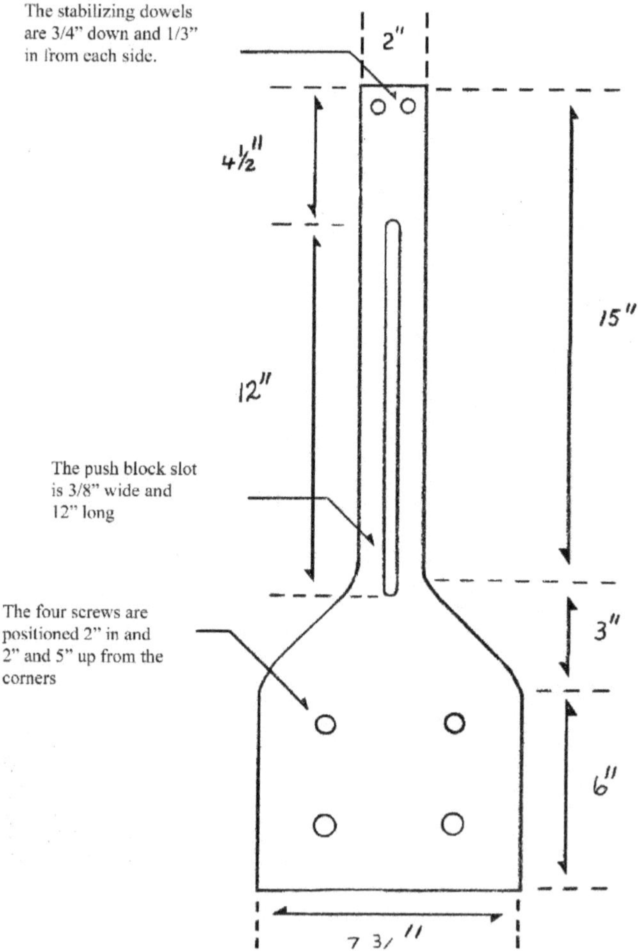

Figure 17 The tower dimensions

Extend the straight lines past the curved areas then use a rounded object to draw in an appropriate arc. Use the band saw to cut the tower perimeter and buff the sharp edges with 120 grit sandpaper.

Figure 18 Drawing in the curved lines

Cut the Press Block and
Press Block Spacer Blanks

The press block consists of 8 pieces of 3/4" MDF and 1 piece of 3/16" plywood cut to the dimensions shown in the figure below. The assembled width of the press block will be 6.1875 inches. This is slightly less than the 6.375 inch width of the main body.

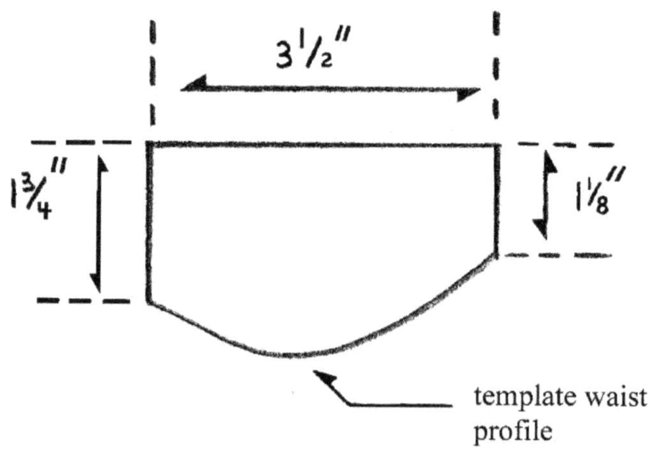

Figure 19 The press block blank profile

Cut a 3" x 30" blank from 3/4" MDF stock. Ensure that one side is true. With a square draw a series of perpendicular lines 3 3/4" apart. Clamp a trued piece of 3/4" stock to a flat work surface. Clamp the blank to the work surface parallel to the first piece leaving a space between them of 4 inches. (Figure 21).

Figure 20 Drawing in the press block waist profile

Figure 21 The trued edge and press block blank spaced 4" apart

Use the soundboard template to draw the push block profile by squaring the centerline of the template with the trued edge. (Figure 20).

With the profile now marked, cut out the first section on the band saw and use this piece as a template to draw in the cut lines for the remaining 7 pieces and the plywood spacer. (Figure 22).

Figure 22 Cutting out the first press block piece

Glue up the Press Block and Trim the Edges

Glue up the 8 pieces with the spacer. Do not use the spacer as one of the outside blocks. The press block surfaces will invariably have minor irregularities. The pieces were intentionally made slightly larger than the finished press block dimensions to allow for the edges to be trued on the table saw.

To give the press block a finished appearance, run the press block through the table saw to sharpen the top and side edges. During this process be sure to maintain the square of the sides and top so that the top remains perpendicular to the push block threaded rod. Note that the original 3 3/4" width of the press block will be reduced.

Figure 23 The press block after gluing and edging

Then, check the block profile with the profile of the main body panel. Note any irregularities and buff them down until a satisfactory fit is obtained. (Figure 24).

Figure 24 Checking the press block for fit

Fabricate and Glue Up the Press Block Channel Extensions

The press block channel extensions guide the press block as it travels up and down the tower channel. Create two press block extension blanks from poplar stock.

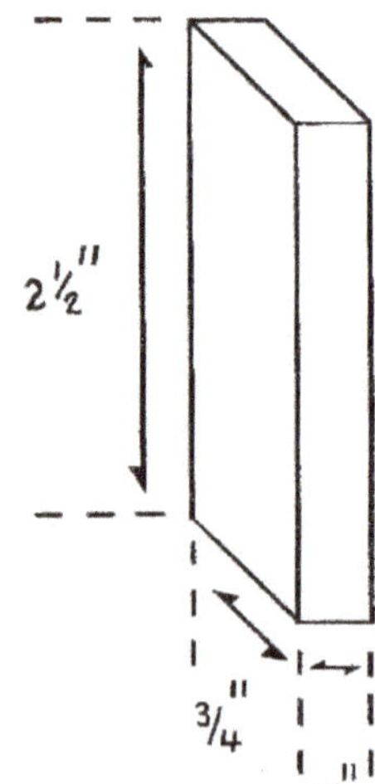

Figure 25 The press block extension blank

The width of the extension should be 3/8" to fit into the 3/8" tower channel. The length should be 3/4" which will be long enough to extend through the tower channel.

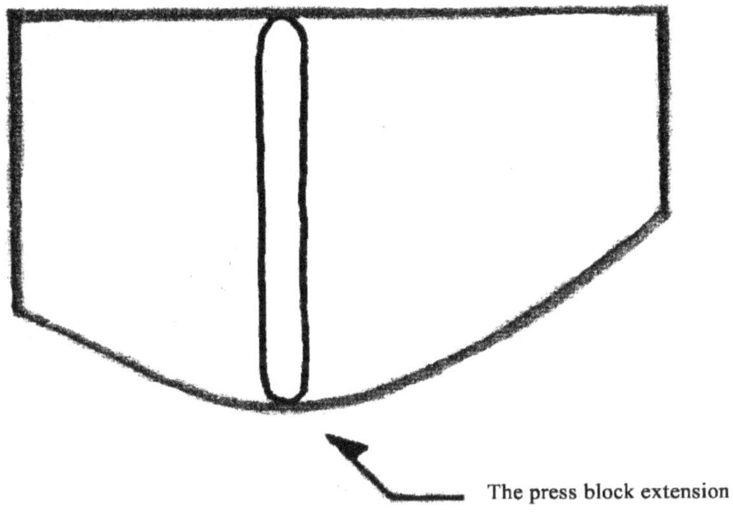

Figure 26 The press block extension diagram

The height should be equal to the height of the block from the valley to the top. You may want to round the top and bottom of the extension, however that is just a personal aesthetic option.

To ensure proper alignment of the press block extensions on the press block, clamp the two towers to the main body panels with the press block channel in line with the lowest point on the main form waist. Place the press block in the form. The top of the press block should be level.

Using the channel edges as a guide, mark two lines on the press block identifying the edges of the channel. The press block extensions will be glued to the press block between these two lines.

Figure 27 Marking the press block extension lines

Remove the press block and glue the extensions to the press block with CA glue and accelerator. Apply the CA glue to the extension's glue surface. If you are using spray accelerator, tape strips of blue painter's tape on both sides of the lines on the press block and apply the accelerator. Then press the pieces together.

Dry Fit the Sides, Main Body, and Press Block

Once the glue for the press block extensions has set, reassemble the towers, main body and press block with the extensions in the channel. It is unlikely that the 3/8" press block extensions, even if precisely fabricated to exact widths, will slide freely in the 3/8" tower channel, therefore fine tune the width of the extensions and slightly widen the channels by lightly sanding any areas that bind until the block moves freely up and down the channel.

Attach the Handle to the 3/4 inch Threaded Rod

Attach the handle to the 3/4" threaded rod with a hex nut and locking nut. Dry fit the three components and note the position of the hex nut then remove the three pieces.

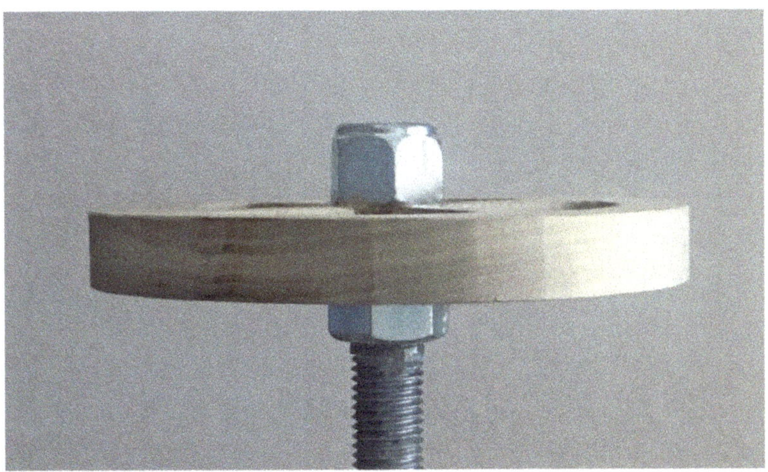

Figure 28 The press block handle assembly

Place a small amount of 2 part epoxy on the threaded rod where the hex nut will be positioned and thread the hex nut onto the threaded rod. Next, place a small amount of epoxy on the threaded rod just above the hex nut and slide the handle onto the rod. Finally, place a small amount of epoxy on the threaded rod where the lock nut will be positioned and thread the lock nut onto the threaded rod. When assembled the threaded rod should be flush with or just proud of the lock nut. Tighten the 3 components and allow the epoxy to set.

Fabricate the Upper Press Block Housing Blanks

The press block assembly provides the pressure applied to the press block. The press block assembly components are: 1) the towers, 2) the 3/4" threaded rod, 3) the press block, 4) 3/4" washer, 5) 3/4" lock nut, 6) the press block top, 7) the upper press block housing, 8) 3/4" hex nut, 9) the handle, and 10) 3/4" lock nut. (Figure 29)

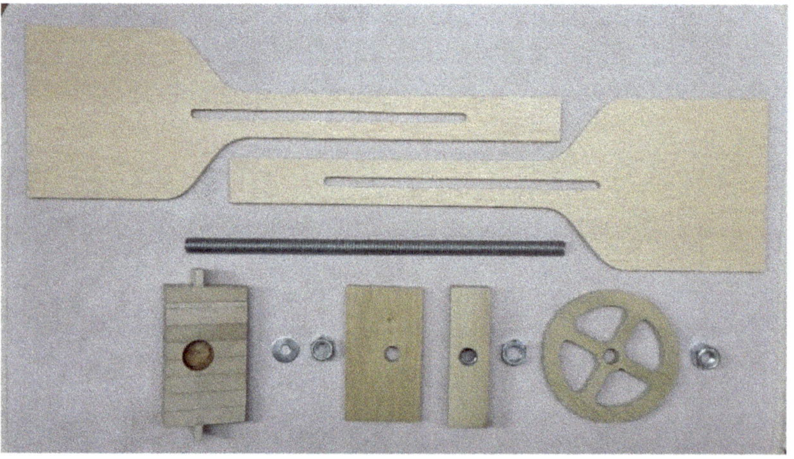

Figure 29 The press block assembly components

The upper press block housing forms the support for the towers and holds the hex nut through which the press block assembly rod passes. Cut two 3/4" x 1 3/4" x 6 1/8" upper press block housing blanks from poplar stock. (Figure30).

26

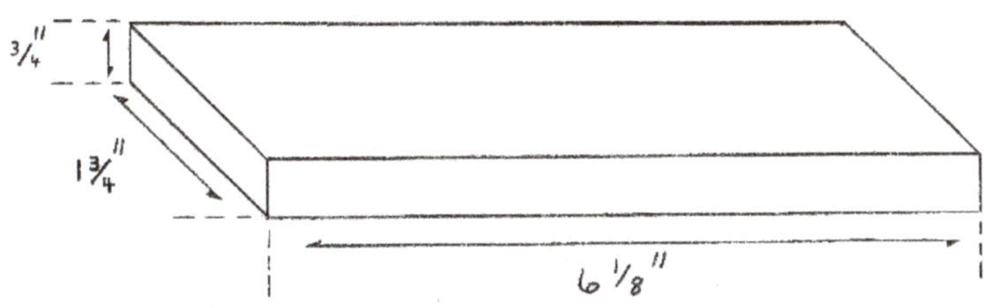

Figure 30 Upper press block housing blank

The threaded rod, passing through the upper press block housing hole will drop straight down and meet the press block at a point directly above the lowest point of the waist.

The threaded rod will not enter the press block cavity in the center. (Figure 31)

Figure 31 The press block showing the threaded rod entering the press block 1 3/8" from the upper bout edge of the press block

27

Mark the Outline of the Hex Nut

Check the upper press block housings for square, then mark the centers. Place the hex nut in the center of one of the two housing halves and mark the outline.

Use a chisel to excavate a cavity for the hex nut equal to half the height of the nut. Repeat this process on the other half. The hex nut will be sandwiched between the two pieces and secured with two part fast drying epoxy.

Figure 32 Excavating the hex nut cavity

It is critical that the hex nut sit level in the cavity with the threads perpendicular to the housing so that the threaded rod and press block will move through the housing and up and down the channel without binding. (Figure 33)

Figure 33 The hex nut sitting level in the cavity

Dry fit the two halves together with the hex nut inserted to make certain the two halves will close. Remove the nut and use a 3/4" brad point bit to drill a hole precisely in the cavity center of each of the housing halves.

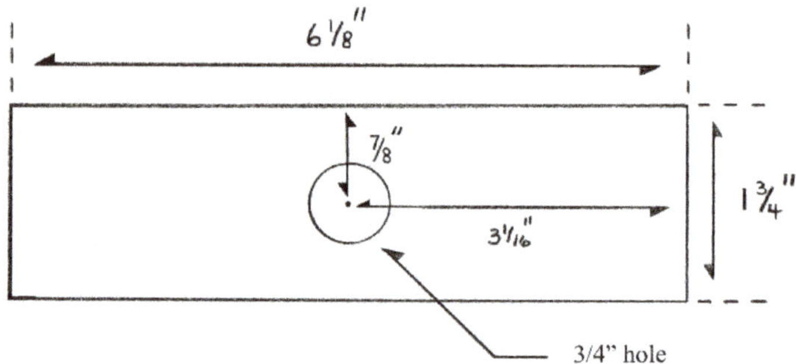

Figure 34 The upper press block dimensions

Cover the top and bottom of the hex nut with blue painter's tape. Coat the cavity walls of the housing to be used as the lower piece with 2 part epoxy and insert the nut. Check the position of the nut in the cavity for vertical and horizontal accuracy relative to the housing. Be careful not to allow any epoxy to enter the center of the nut and interfere with the threads. Allow the epoxy to cure.

Figure 35 Blue tape over the hex nut threads

Glue the two pieces of the upper press block housing together with white glue. (Figure 36)

Figure 36 The upper press block housing glued together with hex nut inserted

Fabricate the Press Block Top

Cut the press block top blank from 3/4" poplar stock. Reduce the 3/1/2" width of the blank to fit the width of the press block as reduced by the finishing process.

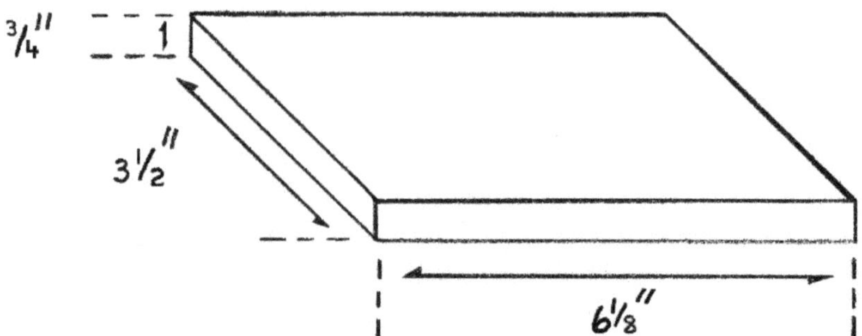

Figure 37 The press block top

Mark the Location Where the Press Rod Will Enter the Press Block Top

The press rod will enter the press block top at a point equidistant from either side and in line with the press block extensions. To determine this point, place the press block top on the press block and draw a line across the press block top connecting the press block extension locations. Mark the center point of this line. Then drill a 3/4" hole for the press block rod.

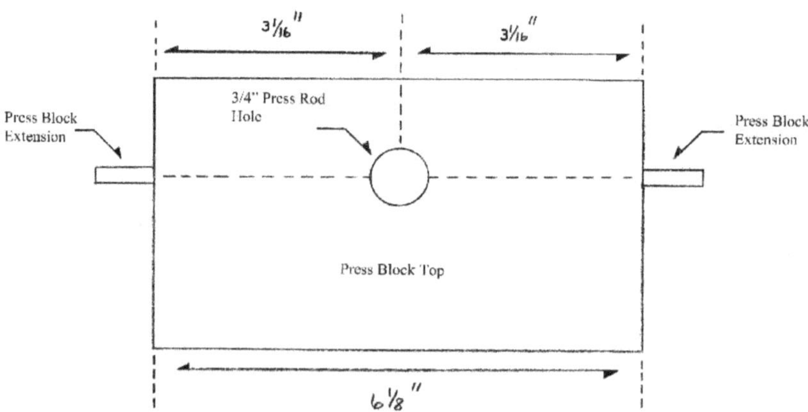

Figure 38 The press block top 3/4" hole location

Excavate the Press Block Cavity

The press block rod passes through the press block top. A lock nut is attached to the end of the press block rod that must turn freely in the press block cavity. A washer is placed on the bottom of the cavity to avoid undue wear on the press block. The lock nut pushes against the washer on the bottom of the press block cavity and the descending push rod provides the pressure to push the wood into the waist of the main body form.

The lock nut is 1" wide and 3/4" tall and the washer approximately 1 1/4" wide and 1/10" thick. Use a 1 1/2" Forstner bit to excavate a cavity 1" deep and 1 1/2" wide to allow the lock nut to turn freely when inserted into the cavity with the press block top in place.

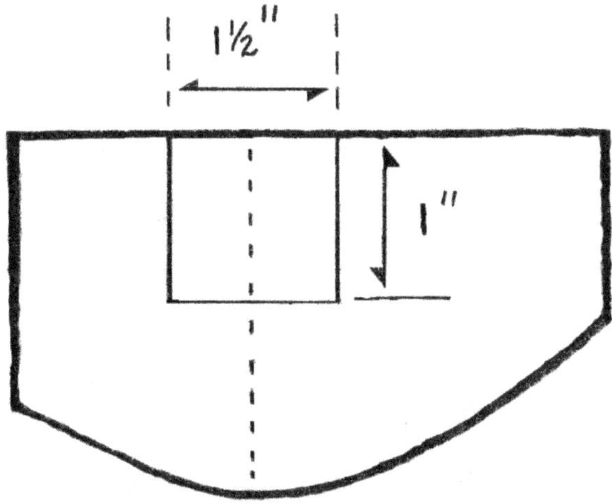

Figure 39 The press block cavity

Insert the washer into the bottom of the press block cavity and secure it with 2 part epoxy. (Figure 39)

Assemble the Press Block Column

The press block column is assembled in the following order on the push rod: 1) the top lock nut (fixed), 2) the handle (fixed), 3) the hex nut (fixed), 4) the upper press block housing, 5) the press block top, 6) the lock nut (fixed). (Figure 40)

Figure 40 The press block column

Attach the lock nut to the bottom of the threaded rod and secure it in place with some 2 part epoxy. The bottom of the lock nut should be flush with the end of the threaded rod.

Glue the Press Block Top to the Press Block

With the press block column assembled, glue the press block top to the press block with white glue and allow to dry.

Dry Fit the Towers and Press Block Column

Clamp the towers to the form with the press block extensions inserted into the channels. Adjust the position of the upper press block housing so that it is even with the tops of the towers. Clamp the upper press block housing in place. Raise and lower the press block by turning the handle and ensure that the press block is able to travel freely up and down the channels. The channels should be exactly perpendicular to the base of the form.

Figure 41 Dry fitting the towers and press block column

Attach the Towers to the Form

Attach the towers to the form with 3/4" screws. The screws are positioned 2" in from either side. The lower screws are 2" up from the bottom and the upper screws are 5 " up from the bottom. (Figure 42).

Figure 42 Tower attached with countersunk screws

Glue in the Upper Press Block Housing

With the towers in place and properly aligned, glue up the upper press block housing.

Figure 43 Gluing in the upper press block housing

Stabilize and Strengthen Upper
Press Block Housing

After the glue has set, add additional strength to the press
block housing glue joint by inserting two 3/8 inch dowels in each side.

Figure 44 Stabilizing dowels

Drill the holes 1 inch deep and glue the dowels in with
white glue. Then flush the dowels even with the sides with a saw
or chisel and sandpaper

Make the Hold Down Handles

The hold down assemblies are bolted to the main body, and with the press block column, serve to apply pressure to the heated wood to conform to the main body profile. The components of the hold down assembly consist of eye bolts, utility knobs, handles, threaded rods, washers, and nuts.

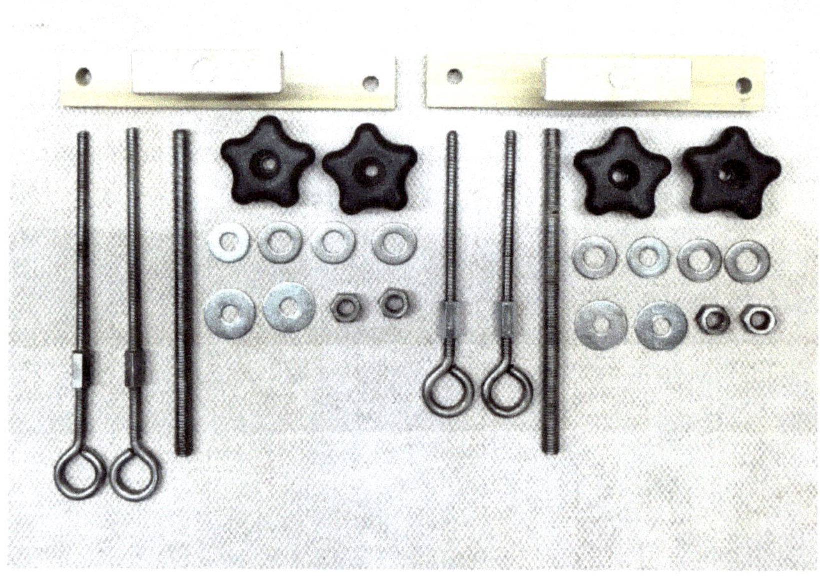

Figure 45 Hold down bar components

The three piece handles, the hold down bar, the connecting dowel, and the hand grip, are easily made from readily available poplar and 1/2" dowel stock.

The hold down bars are cut to dimensions 3/4" x 1 1/4" x 7 3/4".

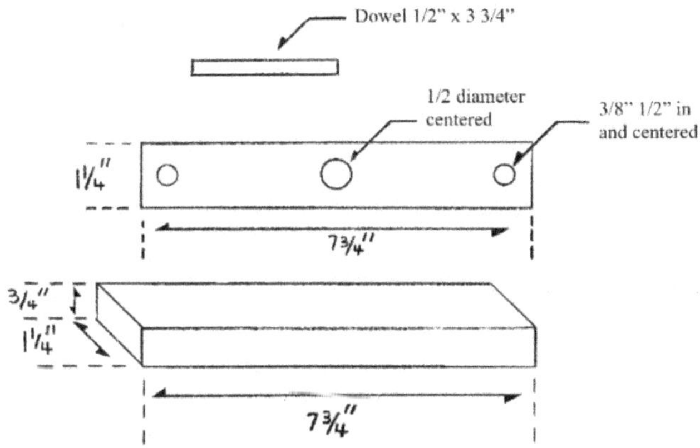

Figure 46 The hold down bar and connecting dowel

The hand grips are cut to 5/8" x 7/8" x 3".

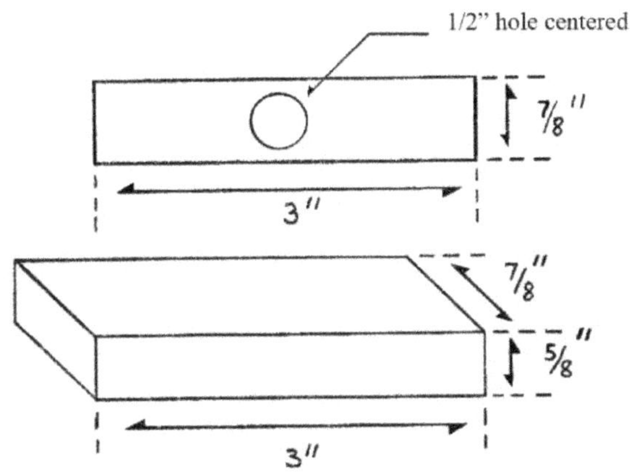

Figure 47 The hand grips

Glue the connecting dowel to the hold down bar with 2 part epoxy and allow to set. Epoxy is used for this step as the heat from the heating blanket may cause the connecting dowel and hold down bar to separate.

Next, glue up the connecting dowel and the handle with white glue. To ensure the handle is straight with the connecting bar during the glue drying process, lay the two pieces on a flat surface and press them down until the handle on the connecting dowel and the hold down bar are parallel.

The hold down assembly is attached to the main body by the threaded rod with the eye bolt sandwiched between two washers and fixed with the nut. The utility knob and washer are then threaded onto the eye bolt extension.

Figure 48 The hold down bar assembly

With the attachment of the hold down bar assembly, the side bending machine should be complete.

Figure 49 The assembled side bending machine

Final Thoughts

The template for the machine described in this book is for an OM or 000 style guitar.   However, the same process can easily be adapted to make a machine for bending the sides of a dreadnought, parlor, or Jumbo. And for those who wish to craft their projects using the metric system, an English/Metric Conversion Chart has been included.

The sturdy design of this side bending machine will be easy to operate, of superior quality, deliver accurate results, and provide years of faithful service for a fraction of the cost of a commercially produced machine.

Happy Bending
William C. Peterson

Table of Figures

Imperial/Metric Conversion Chart

Inches			Metric	
0.031"	1/32"	0.79 mm	1.0 mm	0.039"
0.062"	1/16"	1.57 mm	1.8 mm	0.071"
0.125"	1/8"	3.18 mm	2.0 mm	0.079"
0.188"	3/16"	4.78 mm	3.0 mm	0.118"
0.250"	1/4"	6.35 mm	3.2 mm	0.126"
0.313"	5/16"	7.95 mm	4.0 mm	0.157"
0.375"	3/8"	9.53 mm	4.3 mm	0.169"
0.438"	7/16"	11.13 mm	4.6 mm	0.181"
0.500"	1/2"	12.70 mm	5.0 mm	0.197"
0.563"	9/16"	14.30 mm	6.0 mm	0.236"
0.625"	5/8"	15.88 mm	7.0 mm	0.276"
0.688"	11/16"	17.48 mm	8.0 mm	0.315"
0.750"	3/4"	19.05 mm	9.0 mm	0.354"
0.813"	13/16"	20.65 mm	1.0 cm	0.394"
0.875"	7/8"	22.23 mm	2.0 cm	0.787"
0.938"	15/16"	23.83 mm	3.0 cm	1.181"
1"	1"	2.54 cm	4.0 cm	1.575"
2"	2"	5.08 cm	5.0 cm	1.969"
3"	3"	7.62 cm	6.0 cm	2.362"
4"	4"	10.16 cm	7.0 cm	2.756"

5"	5"	12.70 cm	8.0 cm	3.150"
6"	6"	15.24 cm	9.0 cm	3.543"
7"	7"	17.78 cm	10.0 cm	3.937"
10"	10"	25.40 cm		

Diagrams and Dimensions

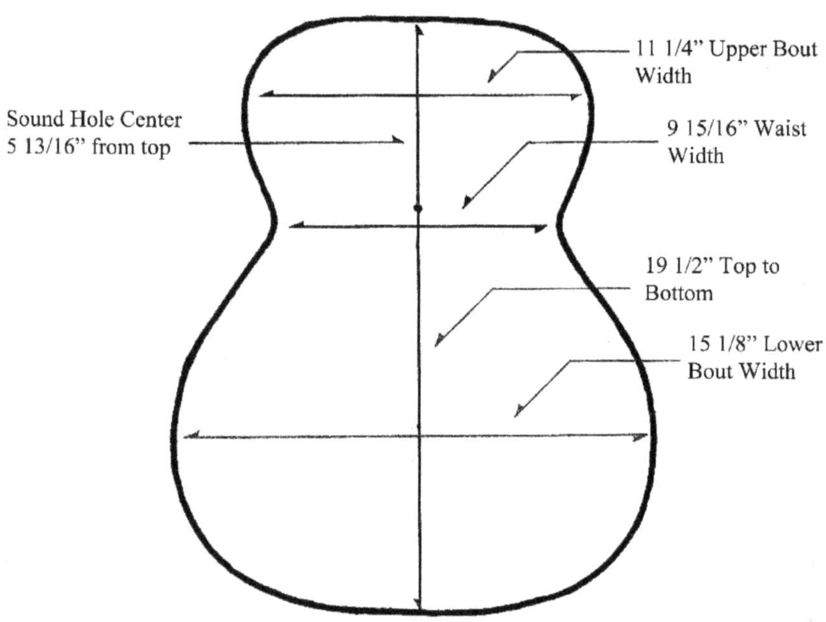

Figure 2

The Guitar Template

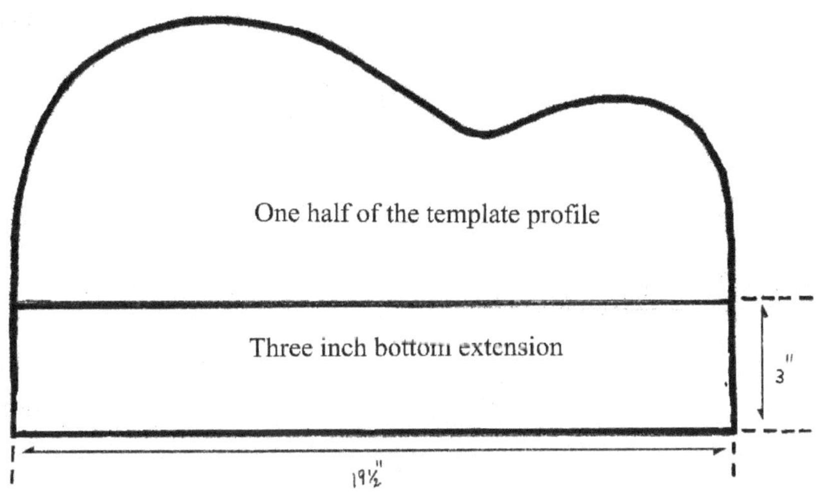

Figure 5

The Main Body Panel Profile

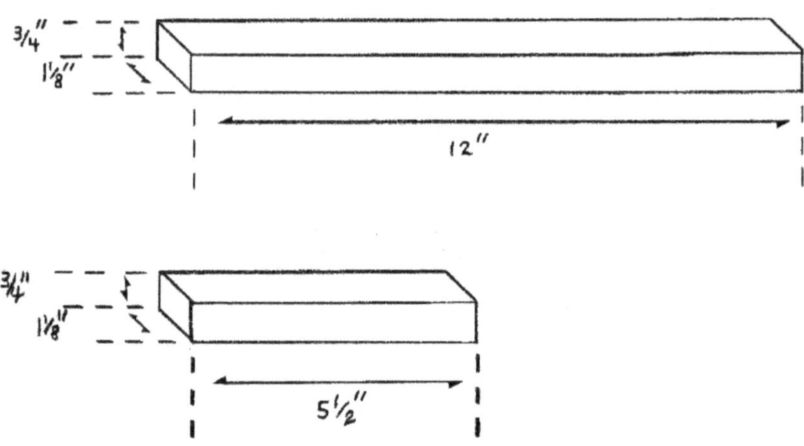

Figure 7

The Long and Short Body Panel Spacers

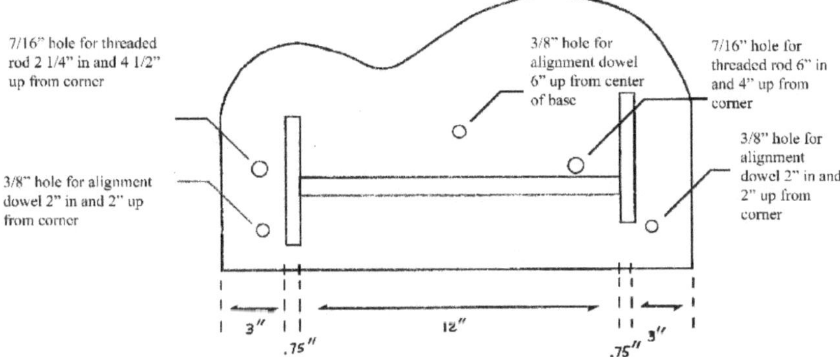

Figure 9

Positions of the Alignment Dowels
and Threaded Rods

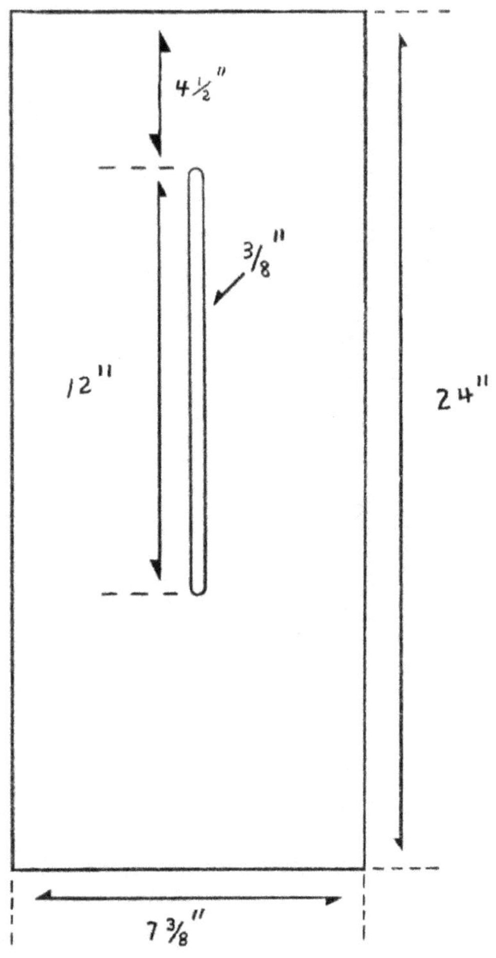

Figure 15

The Tower Blank Dimensions

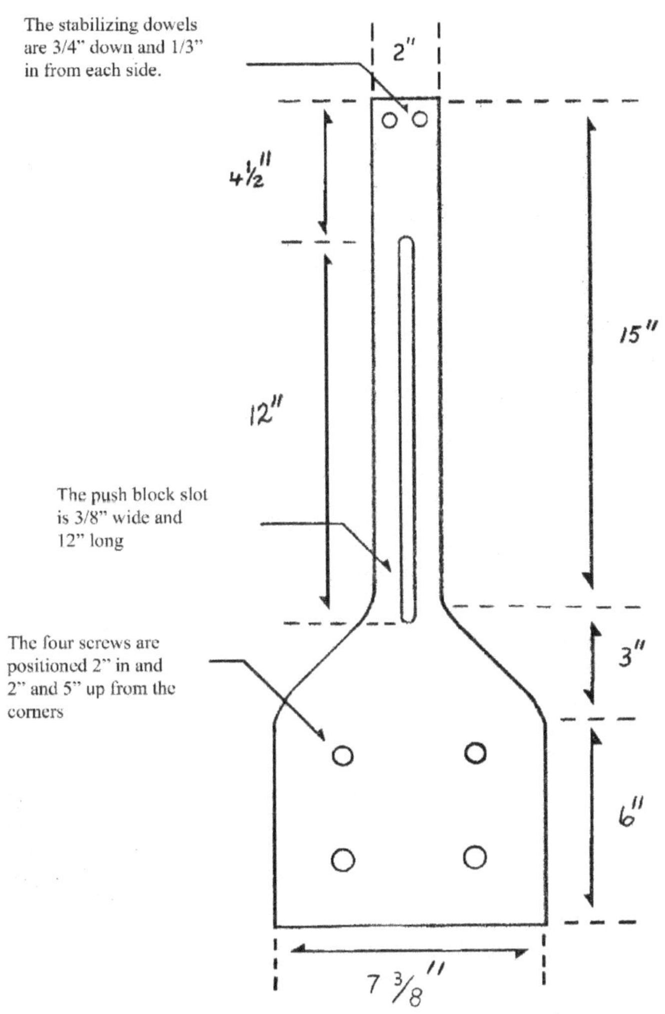

Figure 17

The Tower Dimensions

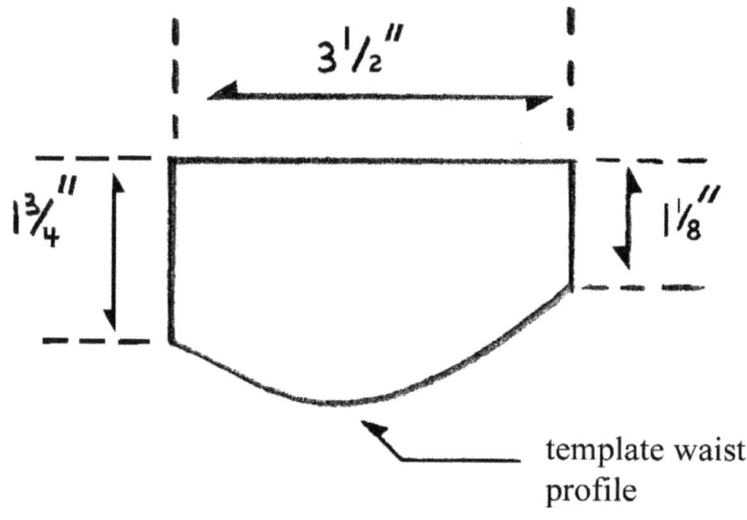

Figure 19

The Press Block Blank Profile

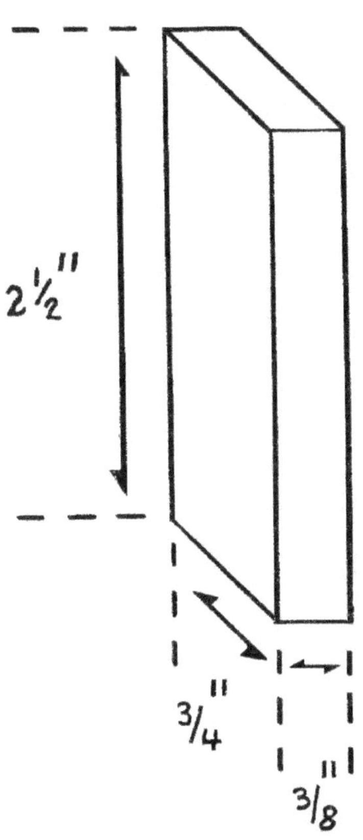

Figure 25

The Press Block Extension Blank

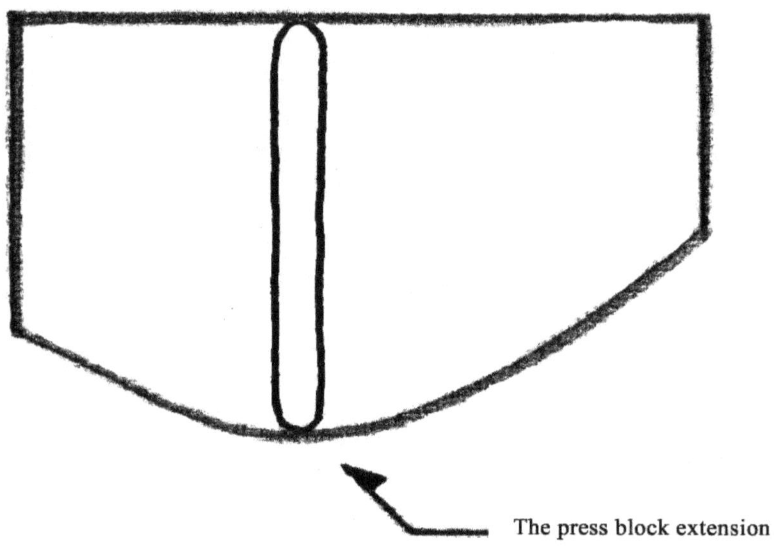

Figure 26

The Press Block Extension Diagram

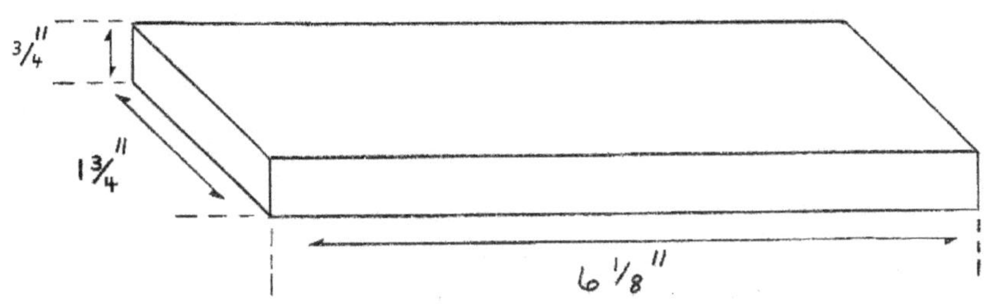

Figure 30

Upper Press Block Housing Blank

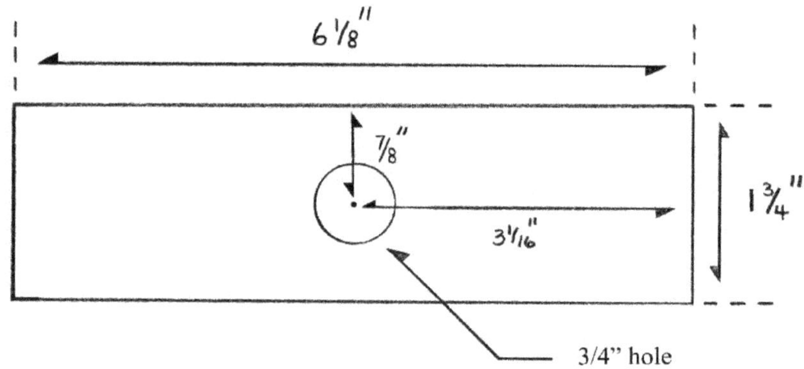

Figure 34

The Upper Press Block Dimensions

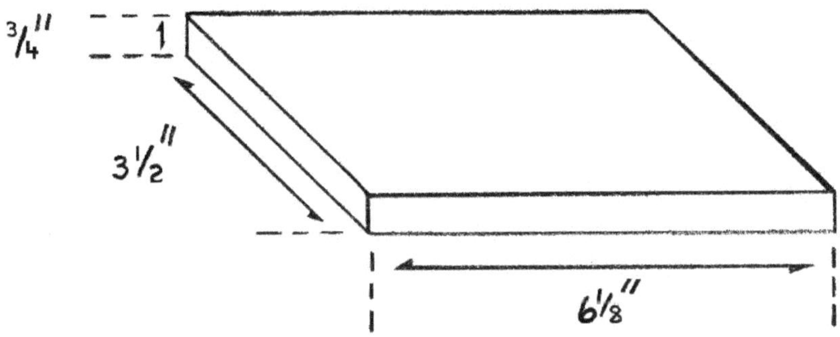

Figure 37

The Press Block Top

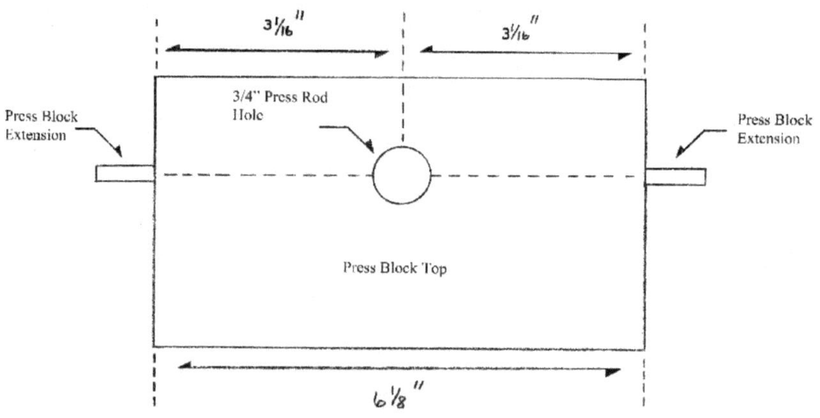

Figure 38

The Press Block Top 3/4" Hole Location

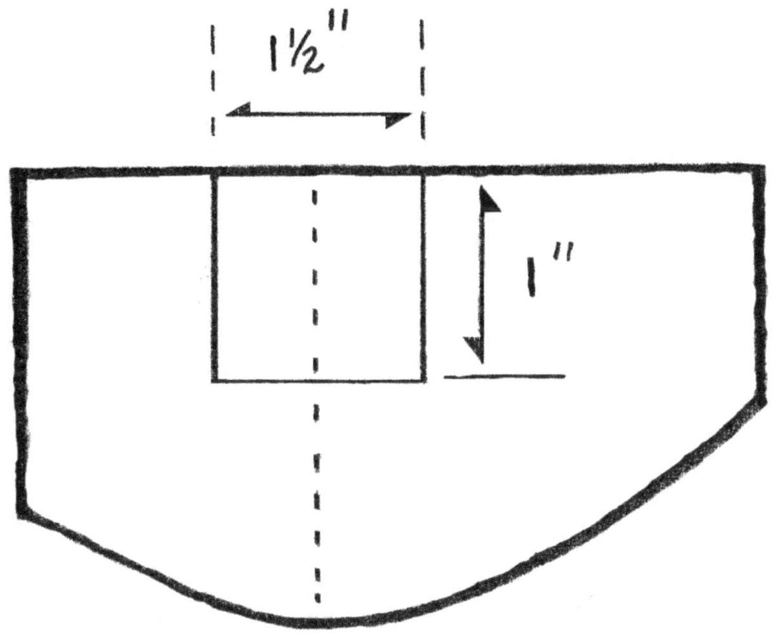

Figure 39

The Press Block Cavity

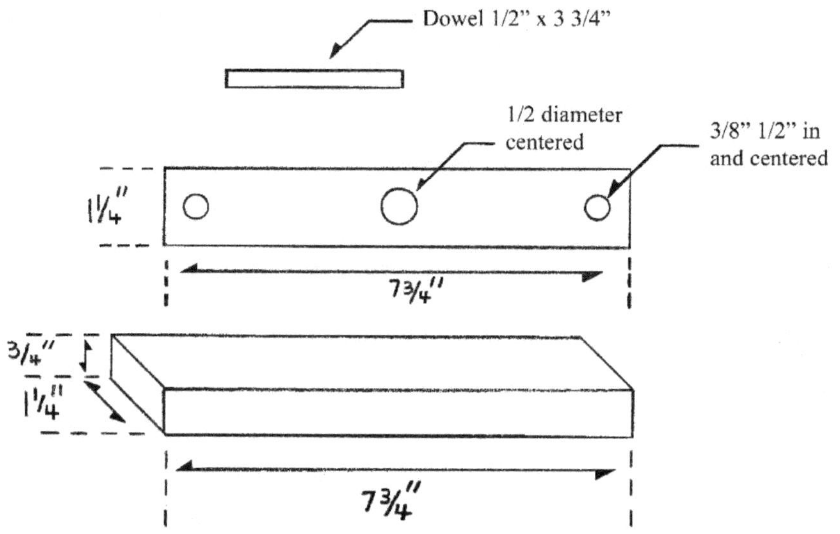

Figure 46

The Hold Down Bar and Connecting Dowel

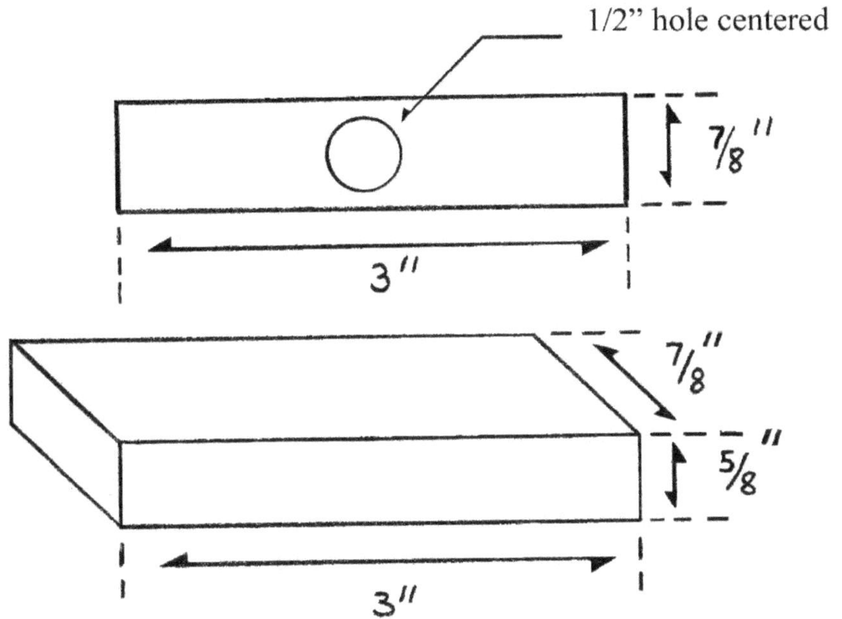

Figure 47

The Hand Grips

About the Author

William C. Peterson is a guitar maker in Round Rock, Texas. He learned guitar making at the Whetstone School of Lutherie in Brattleboro, Vermont under the supervision of master guitar maker Scott Hausmann. He is a member of the Guild of American Luthiers and a retired attorney. He and his wife, Elizabeth, live in Round Rock, Texas.

Notes

Notes